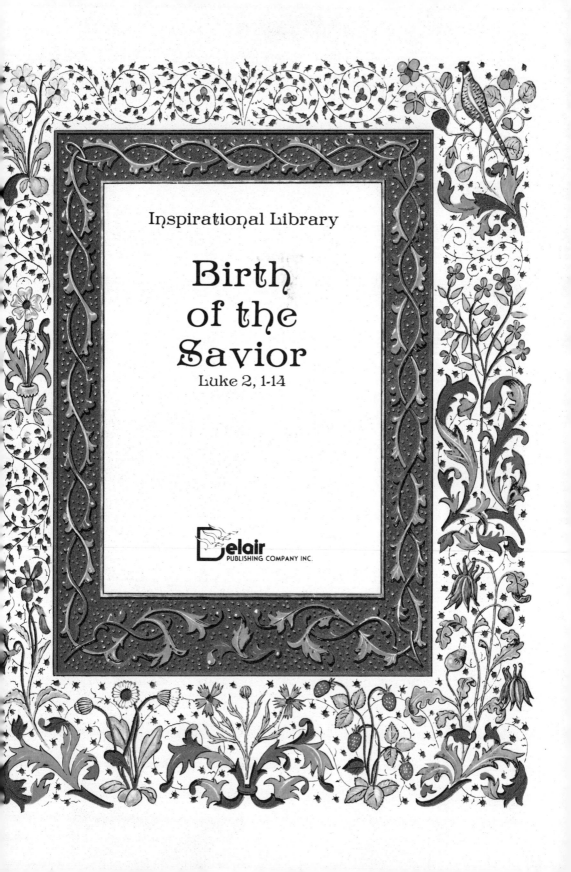

Inspirational Library

Birth of the Savior

Luke 2, 1-14

Belair
PUBLISHING COMPANY INC.

All Scripture passages in this book are according to the
King James Version.

ISBN: 0-8326-2004-1

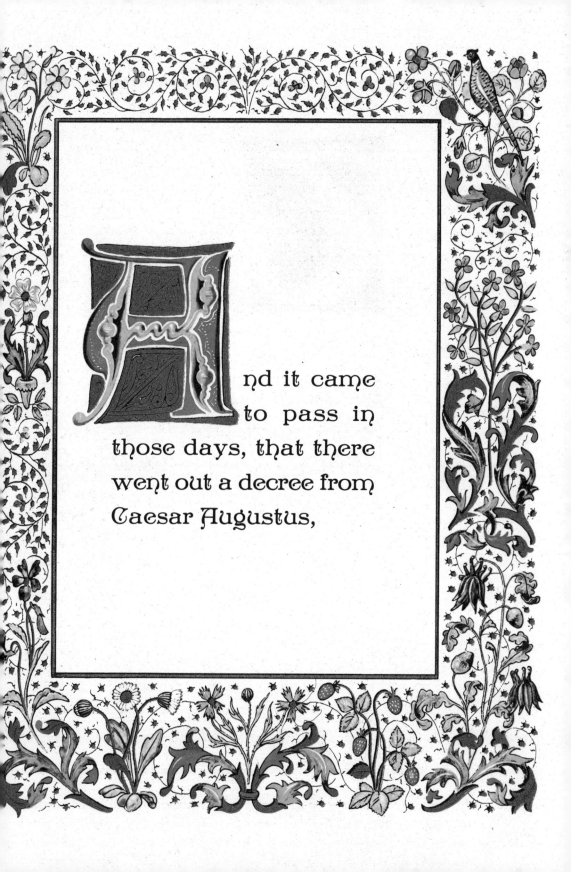

And it came to pass in those days, that there went out a decree from Caesar Augustus,

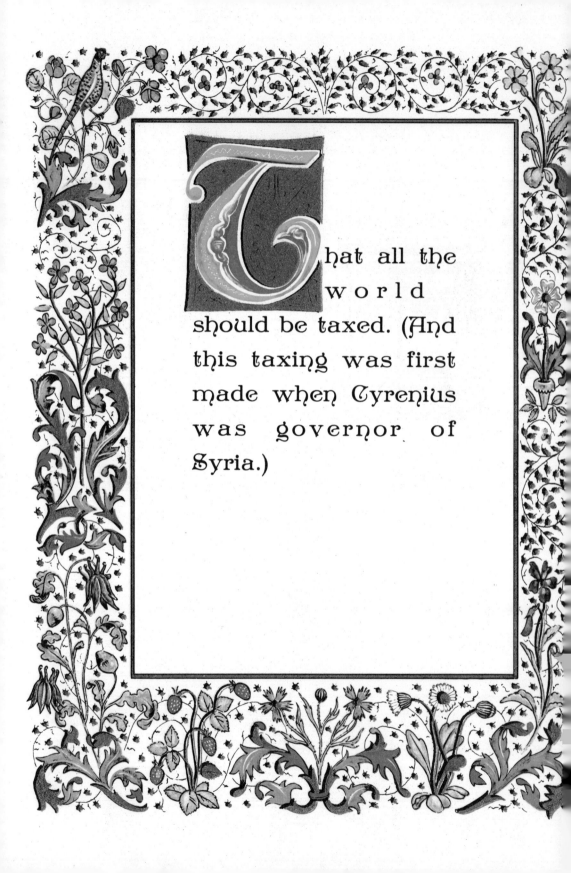

That all the world should be taxed. (And this taxing was first made when Cyrenius was governor of Syria.)

And all went to be taxed, everyone into his own city.

And

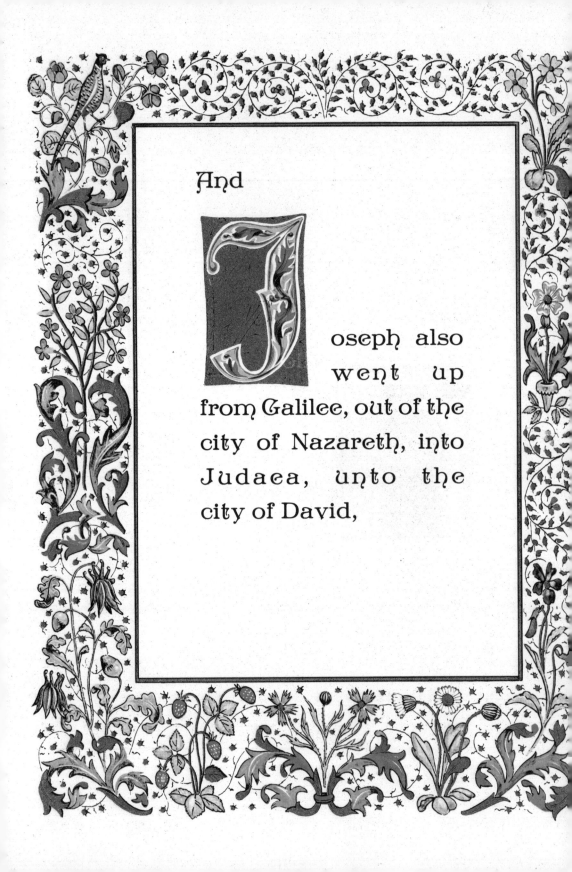

Joseph also went up from Galilee, out of the city of Nazareth, into Judaea, unto the city of David,

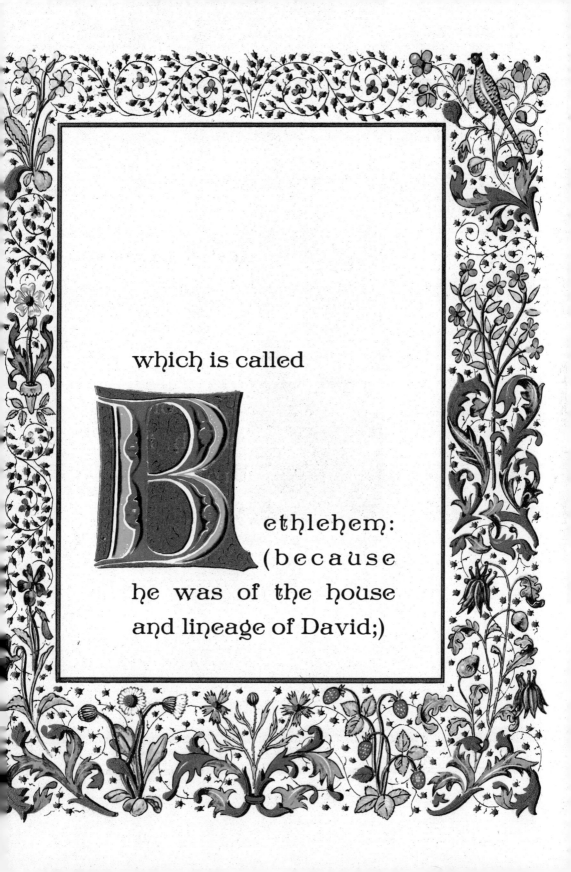

which is called

Bethlehem:
(because
he was of the house
and lineage of David;)

o be taxed with Mary his espoused wife, being great with child.

And so it was, that, while they were there, the days were accomplished that she should be delivered

And she brought forth her firstborn son, and wrapped him in swaddling clothes, and laid him in a manager:

ecause there was no room for them in the inn.

And there were in the same country shepherds abiding in the field, keeping watch over their flock by night. And, lo, the angel of the Lord came upon them, and the glory of the Lord shone round about them; and they were sore afraid.

And the angel said unto them, Fear not; for, behold, I bring you good tidings of great joy, which shall be to all people.

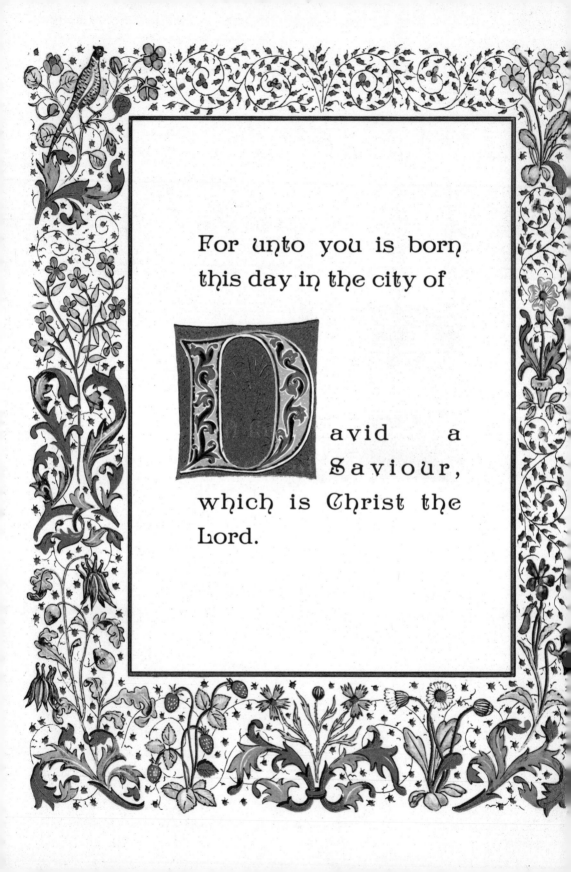

For unto you is born this day in the city of David a Saviour, which is Christ the Lord.

And this shall be a sign
unto you:

Ye shall find
the babe
wrapped in swaddling
clothes, lying in a
manger.

And suddenly there was with the angel a multitude of the heavenly host praising God and saying, Glory to God in the highest, and on earth peace, good will toward men.